A PEANUTS VALENTINE

SHARE THE LOVE WITH THIS
BRAND-NEW COLLECTION
OF VALENTINE'S DAY FAVORITES!

FEB.
14

LOVE
LETTER!

CHARLES M. SCHULZ

BALLANTINE BOOKS • NEW YORK

A Ballantine Book
Published by the Ballantine Publishing Group
Copyright © 2003 United Feature Syndicate, Inc.

www.ballantinebooks.com
www.snoopy.com

Library of Congress Control Number: 2002095783

ISBN 0-345-45941-5

Book design by Diane Hobbing of Snap-Haus Graphics
Cover design by United Media

Manufactured in the United States of America

First Edition: February 2003

2 4 6 8 10 9 7 5 3 1

A
PEANUTS
VALENTINE

8

9

10

PEANUTS

VALENTINES, HUH?

YES, THEY'RE FOR ALL THE BOYS I LIKE IN OUR CLASS AT SCHOOL

WAIT...YOU DROPPED ONE... IT HAS THE INITIALS "C.B." ON IT....

WE WOULDN'T WANT TO LOSE **THAT** ONE, WOULD WE? HA HA HA HA HA HA

NO, I GUESS NOT...CRAIG BOWERMAN WOULD BE VERY DISAPPOINTED.

2-13

PEANUTS

HERE COMES THE MAILMAN WITH ALL THE VALENTINES SENT TO ME BY MY FRIENDS..

I'LL JUST STAND HERE AND LET HIM GIVE THEM TO ME, AND THEN I'LL TAKE THE WHOLE ARMFUL INTO THE HOUSE...

..THEN I'LL OPEN THEM ONE BY ONE, AND.... AND... AND....

SIGH

2-14

12

14

16

17

21

PEANUTS

2-14

PEANUTS

AND I GOT A VALENTINE FROM JOYCE AND I GOT ONE FROM PEGGY

AND I GOT ONE FROM ZELMA, AND JANELL, AND BOOTS AND PAT, AND SYDNEY, AND WINNIE, AND JEAN, AND ROSEMARY, AND COURTNEY, AND FERN, AND MEREDITH ...

AND AMY, AND JILL, AND BETTY, AND MARGE, AND KAY, AND FRIEDA, AND ANNABELLE, AND SUE, AND EVA, AND JUDY, AND RUTH ...

AND BARBARA, AND OL' HELEN, AND ANN, AND JANE, AND DOROTHY, AND MARGARET, AND...

I CAN'T STAND IT... I JUST CAN'T STAND IT...

2-15

24

27

39

41

43

44

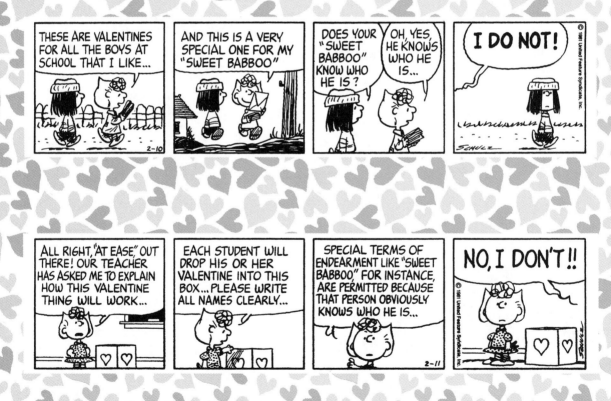

48

50

51

53

54

56

57

63

64

69

71

75

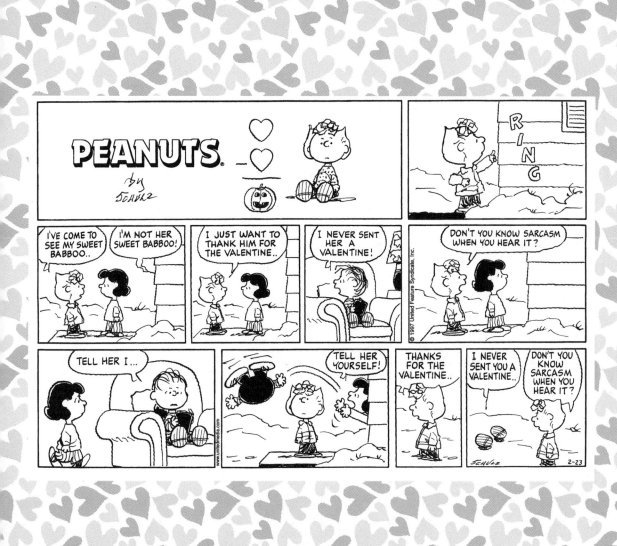

IT'S A VALENTINE FOR OUR TEACHER.. SEE? I DREW A GREAT BIG HEART..

IT LOOKS MORE LIKE A BAKED POTATO..

SHE'S A VEGETARIAN.. I'LL DRAW SOME CARROTS AND BROCCOLI AROUND IT..

91

92

GN
J
SCH

185727